1

The animals had their own spirits.

3

Some people lived near the sea.

5

The people saw spirits in sea animals.

7

The turtle was special to some people.

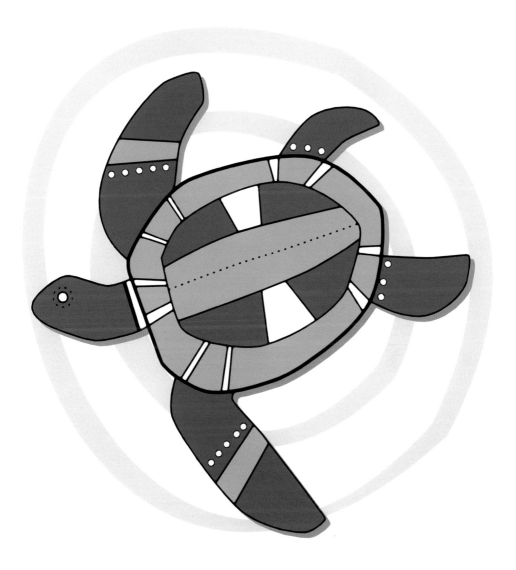

9

It was their totem when they were born.

11

The totem is there to look after
you.

13

You must never hurt the totem.

15

Never go to where the totem forbids.

17

The totem can let you marry
only certain people.

19

We have drawings of the totem.

21

We have stories about the turtle.

23

Word bank

animals

spirits

people

turtle

totem

after

forbids

certain

drawings

stories